This castle is hundreds of years old. No one lives in it anymore. There is no glass in the windows, the walls are broken, and all the roofs have fallen in.

Long, long ago, during the Middle Ages, the castle was new. It was built by a rich man, the lord of the castle. He built it to protect his family, his servants, and his friends. In times of war they stayed safely behind the castle's closed doors and strong, thick walls.

The castle was the lord's home. Inside the walls he and his family could live as they pleased. In times of peace the castle was full of music and laughter. It was a happy place to live.

From up close the old castle looks very big. And it still looks strong. How did people attack it in the Middle Ages?

Did they climb over the walls with a ladder? Did they dig a hole under the walls? Or did they force their way through the front door?

bridge over ditch

All around the castle was a deep ditch. In the Middle Ages the bridge over the ditch could be lifted up to stop anyone from crossing it. That was one way to keep out the enemy.

In front of the doors there were grooves in the walls. An iron grate, or portcullis, slid down the grooves to make a gate. Then came the doors. In back of the doors there were holes in the walls. Wooden bars were put in the holes to keep the doors closed.

portcullis grooves

door

The people inside the castle tried to stop the enemy soldiers by shooting arrows at them and by dropping heavy stones on their heads.

battlement

A winding staircase led to the
top of the tower. From there
soldiers could shoot at the
enemy. But how did they do it
without leaning out and
getting shot themselves? They
hid behind the battlements and
shot through a narrow window
called an arrow loop.

battlement

Below the battlements were
holes. Sometimes beams were
pushed through the holes.

arrow loop

wooden
hoarding

Small wooden scaffolds called
hoardings were built on top of
the beams.

13

There were many wars in the Middle Ages, and soldiers found more and more ways to get into castles. So the castle people built several lines of walls and towers, one inside the other. Then the defenders could retreat from one line to the next if the enemy forced them back. Right in the middle was the biggest and safest building of all. This was called the lord's keep.

If enemy soldiers got over these walls, where would we go next?

15

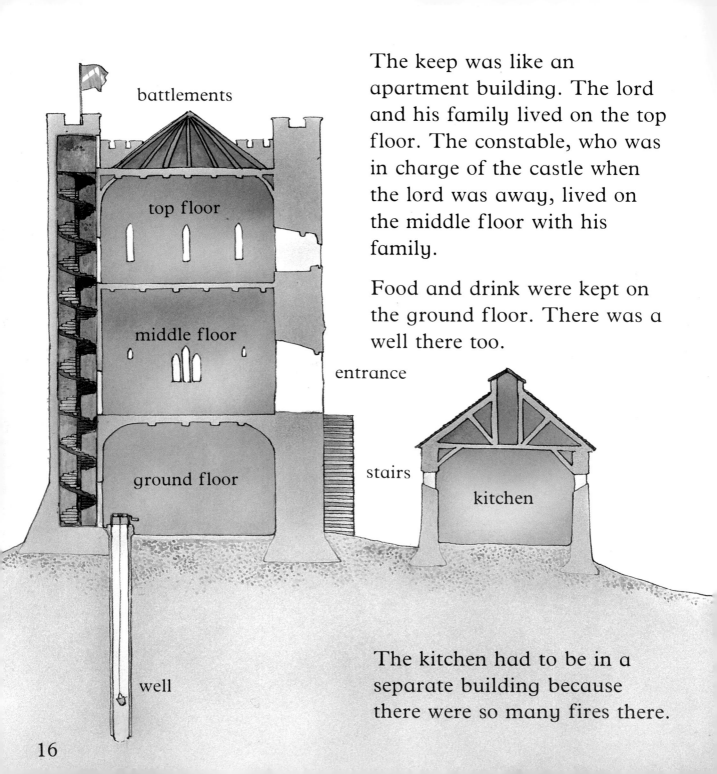

battlements

top floor

middle floor

ground floor

well

entrance

stairs

kitchen

The keep was like an apartment building. The lord and his family lived on the top floor. The constable, who was in charge of the castle when the lord was away, lived on the middle floor with his family.

Food and drink were kept on the ground floor. There was a well there too.

The kitchen had to be in a separate building because there were so many fires there.

16

**THE KEEP**

**Top floor**
Lord's room, great hall, chapel

**Middle floor**
Constable's room, hall, chapel

**Ground floor**
Stores of food, cellars for wine, well, weapons

In the keep the walls were made of stone, but the floors were made of wood. In the Middle Ages there were rugs and straw mats on the floors. The walls were painted white and hung with beautiful cloth and tapestries. The toilets were small rooms with chutes going down inside the walls to smelly pits filled with straw. They had to be emptied by the servants.

Every morning the servants opened the shutters, lit the fire, and pulled back the bed curtains. The servants slept in the same room as the lord and his wife, the lady. When the servants got up, they pushed their beds under the lord's bed. For breakfast there was beer and bread with meat or fish.

After breakfast the lord went to his private chapel. The chapel was the most beautiful room in the keep because the castle builders decorated it to please God. The lord of the castle kept all his business papers and money in the chapel, since it was the most private place in the whole castle.

After prayers the lord and lady often went hunting. Sometimes the lord met other lords in the great hall to discuss politics or to plan for the next war. The kitchen servants spent the day getting dinner ready. The fireplaces had to be big enough to roast a pig or a cow. There were no freezers, so in winter all the meat and fish was salted to keep it from going bad.

Late in the afternoon everyone went to the great hall for dinner. The food was carried in to the sound of trumpets. There were many different types of food: roast swan, fish pie, duckling stuffed with nuts, candy castles made of marzipan. The food was put on thick slices of bread instead of plates.

The castle was like a small town. More than one hundred people worked and lived there, but only a few were women. Nearly all the work in the castle was done by men.

23

There were also many horses, hounds, and
hawks in the castle. The horses were the most
important animals. Castle people could not
manage without them. Knights rode horses when
they went into battle. Messengers on horseback
carried all the lord's letters. And the lord and
lady rode horses when they went hunting.

24

Hawks were also used for hunting. They caught other birds and small animals. Down in the castle yard was a building called the mews, where the hawks were kept. It takes a long time to train a hawk. The man who took care of them was called the falconer.

The lord's prisoners were kept in a dungeon. If a prisoner was rich he could pay a ransom and get out. But if he was poor he had to stay and was treated badly.

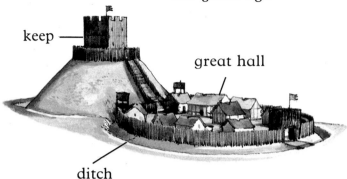

wood and dirt castle, 800 years ago

keep

great hall

ditch

The Middle Ages lasted from about 1100 to 1500. As time passed, people figured out ways to make castles better and stronger. So they kept building new types of castles.

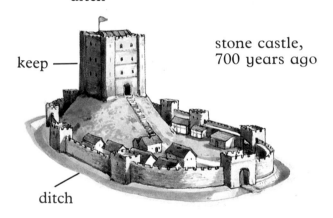

stone castle, 700 years ago

keep

ditch

The first castles were built of wood and dirt. Castles like this were cheap and easy to build. Later castles were built of stone. It took longer and it was more expensive to build stone castles, but they were much stronger and much safer.

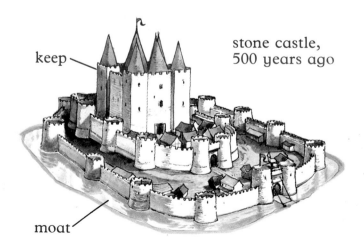

stone castle, 500 years ago

keep

moat

Some castles had round towers and some had square towers. Some had dry ditches around them. Some had moats full of water. Every castle was a different shape and size.

Lords wanted large castles to show how important they were. But not every lord could afford a big castle with lots of walls and towers.

a poor lord's castle

a rich lord's castle

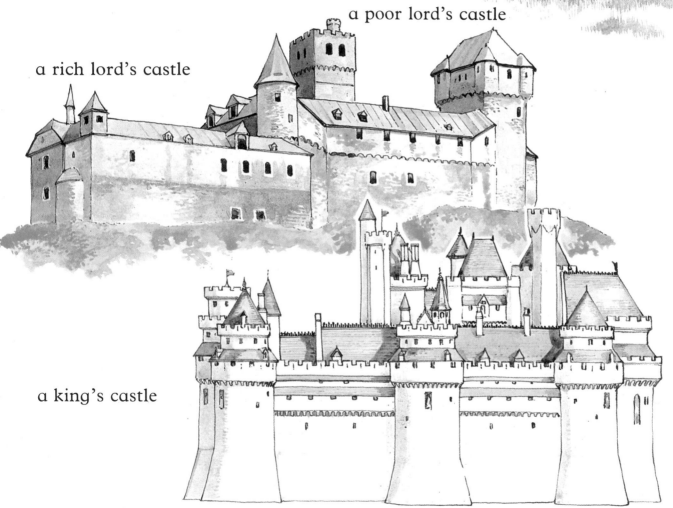

a king's castle

Gradually people found new ways of attacking castles. They invented new weapons. The most important new weapon was the gun. With a really big gun soldiers could knock down the walls and towers. Then the castle people had to surrender.

People began to get tired of fighting all the time. The lords got better at settling arguments peacefully, so they no longer needed castles. They wanted to live in more comfortable houses with bigger windows and more rooms.

When the lords and ladies moved away to their comfortable new houses, the old castles were left empty and deserted. Nobody took care of them. Gradually people forgot about them.

four hundred years ago

one hundred years ago

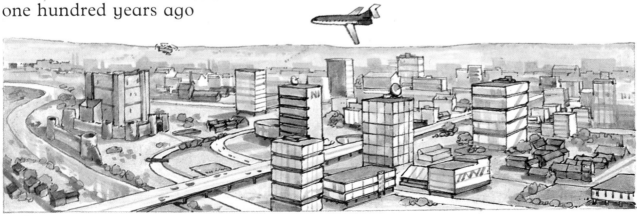

today

Today the old castle sits on its hill. It's just an old ruin, empty and quiet. The furniture, the tapestries on the walls, and the castle people themselves have all vanished.

But people can look at the great hall, the lord's keep, and the empty fireplaces in the kitchens. They can touch the stones that have fallen from the windows. They can imagine the horses and the hawks and all the castle people in their colorful clothes. Long ago this was their home.

I had to leave the wretched creatures to the one surviving stretcher bearer and lead the faithful few who remained and who collected round me away from the fatal spot. Half an hour before I had been at the head of a first-rate company at fighting strength. Now the few who followed me through the maze of trenches where I lost my way were utterly crestfallen [discouraged]. A young lad, a milksop [weak or ineffectual person], who a few days before had been jeered at by his companions because during training he had burst into tears over the weight of a box of ammunition, was now loyally hulking one along on our painful way after retrieving it from the scene of our disaster. When I saw that, I was finished. I threw myself on the ground and broke into convulsive sobs, while the men stood gloomily round me.

Ernst Junger, *Storm of Steel; from the Diary of a German Storm-Troop Officer on the Western Front*. Trans. by Basil Creighton. Garden City, NY: Doubleday, Doran, 1929, pp. 245–46.

# Celebration over the War's End

*Sergeant Tom Grady of the U.S. Army learned of the war's end while he and his fellow soldiers* were in the middle of a battle. Here, Grady remembers the joy he felt on learning that the fighting was over.

*11 November [1918]—Monday*
Cold and raining. Runner in at 10.30 with order to cease firing at 11.00 a.m. Firing continued and we stood by. 306th Machine-Gun Company on my right lost twelve men at 10.55, when a high explosive landed in their position. At 11.00 sharp the shelling ceased on both sides and we don't know what to say. Captain came up and told us that the war was over. We were dumbfounded and finally came to and cheered—and it went down the line like wildfire. I reported Jones' death and marked his grave. Captain conducted a prayer and cried like a baby. Built a big fire and dried our clothes and the bully beef [canned beef] tasted like turkey. We told the new boys our tales and about the battles and they were heavy listeners. Other teams returned from outposts and we celebrated by burning captured ammunition and everything that would burn.

Quoted in "A Soldier's Life" file. Lyn MacDonald, ed., *1914–1918: Voices & Images of the Great War.* New York: Atheneum, 1988, pp. 313–14.

Third Liberty Loan Campaign BOY SCOUTS OF AMERICA

# The Home Front

In addition to soldiers fighting on the battle fronts of World War I, civilians were said to be contributing to the war on the "home front." The large scale of World War I put enormous demands on nations to supply their armed forces with massive numbers of able-bodied soldiers, weapons, equipment, and food. The home front experience was different for each nation. For example, Germany, France, and Great Britain completely reshaped their economies to produce goods for the war, but in Russia, the pressures of shifting to a wartime economy led to a 1917 revolution.

When America entered the war in 1917, the U.S. government led a campaign to bring the country's entire economy behind the war effort. Railroads were nationalized, and the War Industries Board was established to coordinate wartime industrial production. Food and fuel were rationed. Public relations campaigns reminded Americans that "Food is

ammunition—don't waste it" and encouraged people to save leftovers and to have "meatless Tuesdays" and "porkless Thursdays."

Public relations campaigns also encouraged Americans to support the war effort in general. These campaigns used propaganda—official information that uses exaggerations and sometimes outright lies to persuade people to a certain point of view. Led by the federal Committee on Public Information, from 1917 to 1918 the U.S. government organized more than 750,000 speeches on the importance of supporting the military draft, buying war bonds, and volunteering for the Red Cross and other agencies.

In addition to encouraging support for the war effort, the government also suppressed dissenting points of view. Many Americans opposed U.S. entry into the war. Some were pacifists; others were socialists who felt that the war exploited workers. In 1917 and 1918, Congress passed

## FEED a FIGHTER
### Eat only what you need—
### *Waste nothing*—
### That he and his family may have enough

*The war effort included posters urging Americans to consider the needs of soldiers.*

the Espionage Act and the Sedition Act, which together made it a crime to oppose the war effort, although after the war, the Supreme Court ruled that both laws were unconstitutional.

Patriotism and sacrifice; propaganda and political repression—these were the realities of life on the U.S. home front during World War I. The documents in this chapter are intended to expose readers to the variety of ways in which the war transformed the lives of American civilians.

## The Germans Sweep Through Belgium

*During the third week of the opening campaign of World War I in the West, American war correspondent Richard Harding Davis described the onslaught of the German army in its march through Brussels, the capital of officially neutral Belgium. Davis's account was purposely crafted to shape the reaction of American readers in favor of the Allies.*

The Entrance of the German army into Brussels has lost the human quality. It was lost as soon as the three soldiers who led the army bicycled into the Boulevard du Regent and asked the way to the Gare du Nord. When they passed the human note passed with them.

What came after them, and twenty-four hours later is still coming, is not men marching, but a force of nature like a tidal wave, an avalanche or a river flooding its banks. At this moment it is rolling through Brussels as the swollen waters of the Concemaugh Valley swept through Johnstown [referring to the massive flood of Johnstown, Pennsylvania, flood in 1889].

At the sight of the first few regiments of the enemy we were thrilled with interest. After three hours they had passed in one unbroken steel gray column [and] we were bored. But when hour after hour passed and there was no halt, no breathing time, no open spaces in the ranks, the thing became uncanny, inhuman. You returned to watch it, fascinated. It held the mystery and menace of fog rolling toward you across the sea.

The gray of the uniforms worn by both officers and men helped this air of mystery. Only the sharpest eye could detect among

*German soldiers dress in their distinctive gray uniforms.*